YOUR MOROCCAN COOKBOOK

Hassan Erraji

THE SPECIFICS OF THE FOOD CULTURE IN MOROCCO

INTRODUCTION

Moroccan cuisine is one of the most diverse and sumptuous food experiences you will ever have. Moroccan cuisine has developed over thousands of years. It has been influenced and developed from a multitude of cultures such as Arab, Jewish, Iberian, Mediterranean African, Moorish, and the Middle East. Moroccan Cuisine has been refined by the royal kitchens in Marrakech, Titwan, Fez, Meknes, and Rabat.

There is nothing in this world like Moroccan spices. Over the years, there have been many cultures and refugees from a variety of countries that have settled in Morocco, bringing with them spices and many traditional dishes. This led to a vast amount of blended cuisines and spices. The most unique characteristics of this blend are recipes that cook fruit with meat, for example chicken and apricots.

Another great characteristic of Moroccan cuisine is all the Mediterranean vegetables and fruits used in recipes. It is truly unique that the country has been able to use what is produced locally and have done so for generations. Morocco also has fish, poultry, and cattle in abundance, and the availability of these food sources has been a large influence on the country's cuisine.

Moroccan spices can be found in souks and at grocers available almost all throughout the country, the larger souks in larger cities like Agadir, Casablanca, Marrakech, Rabat Fez, Meknes and many others have a wider choice. Here you can find spices in many colors and for rendering different tastes. These flavors and aromas will remain and live with you forever! Many of the Moroccan spices have been imported from other countries and some come locally from Morocco itself. Spices such as saffron come from Taliwin, lemons and oranges from Fez, and olives and mint from Meknes.

The midday meal is the most important meal of the day in Morocco. The midday meal will start with either a hot or cold salad, followed by tagine (sometimes spelled tajine) which is a slow-cooked stew. Bread is always included in the midday meal. This will be followed by either a lamb or chicken dish and then couscous topped with meat and vegetables. It is traditional to finish off the meal with several cups of sweet mint tea.

Couscous is considered a main dish in Morocco, even though it is thought to have originated in the Berber cuisine. Beef is most commonly consumed as the main source of meat, as it is cheaper than lamb. Chicken and turkey are very popular too, and widely consumed by lower budget families and individuals. Seafood is becoming more popular as well, and it is slowly forming an important part of Moroccan cuisine.

Desserts are essential, too, and are not forgotten in Moroccan cuisine! Not all Moroccan desserts are sweet, however. One of the most common desserts is Kaab Ghzal (gazelle's horns). This is a pastry covered in sugar, and stuffed with almond paste. Honey cakes are also very popular; these are made from dough that is deep fried and dipped into hot honey and sprinkled with sesame seeds.

Moroccan cuisine has such incredible variety and great flavors. It is a must for anyone who has a sense of adventure, so let's get started adding some flavor to your meals the Moroccan way!

RECIPES

STARTERS AND APPETIZERS

SERROUDA - MOROCCAN CHICKPEA PUREE

Ingredients

- 400 g dried chickpeas or, if already prepared, approximately 1150 g soaked/peeled chickpeas
- 60ml olive oil (optional)
- One onion, coarsely chopped
- 4 g salt
- 3 g pepper
- pinch of saffron and pinch of turmeric
- cumin to taste
- extra salt and pepper to taste
- paprika to taste

Preparation

1. If you have dried chickpeas, you'll need to place the chickpeas to soak overnight or for at least eight hours in a large bowl with water. Once they have soaked, drain them and remove the skin.
2. Place the chickpeas in a small pot along with the onion, olive oil, and spices. To this add 750ml of water and bring to a boil. Cover, reduce the heat, and simmer the mixture for around 1 1/2 hours.
3. Cool the mixture and puree it in a food processor until smooth. Add additional water as needed to yield a dip that can just barely be poured. If you wish, add additional salt and pepper.
4. Serve the *serrouda* warm as a dip, side dish, or with dinner with bread for dipping. You can add a bit of olive oil, paprika, and cumin as garnish and as extra seasoning.

SPICY KEFTA BRIWATS MOROCCAN FRIED PASTRIES WITH SPICY GROUND BEEF FILLING

Ingredients:

- 45ml olive oil
- Three cloves of garlic, finely chopped
- One green pepper, finely chopped
- 500 g ground meat (beef, lamb, or a combination)
- 6 g chili powder
- 6 g pepper
- 6 g cumin
- One onion, finely chopped
- 6 g paprika
- One tomato, finely chopped
- 3 g salt
- One jalapeno pepper, finely chopped
- 10 ml tomato paste

Ingredients necessary for the Briwats

- For the frying part, you can use vegetable oil
- 60ml melted butter
- One egg yolk, lightly beaten
- 500g warqa, fillo dough, or large spring roll wrappers

Preparation process

1. Heat up the olive oil at medium heat with a frying pan. Take 5 minutes to saute the green peppers and onions.
2. This step consists of adding the garlic, tomatoes, and meat. Keep cooking at medium heat, stirring to divide the meat into several small pieces, to the moment when the meat is thoroughly heated.
3. Mix the meat prices with the jalapeno pepper. Next, stir in the tomato paste, covering all the meat, and keep on cooking for a couple of minutes to combine the flavors.
4. Fold the briwats in this step. Cut the pastry dough into strips around 5 centimeters wide by using scissors. Put one strip of warqa or spring roll wrapper (or 2 layered strips of phyllo dough) over your working surface. Brush the butter on the bottom. Put a big tablespoon of filling near the bottom of the strip, and fold the bottom up to enclose the filling.
5. Align the bottom left corner of the enclosed dough with the right edge of the strip by folding it upwards to the right. The next step would be to align the bottom right corner with the left edge of the dough by flipping it upwards to the left. In the end, you will need to obtain a triangle. Keep on folding the triangle in the same manner until you reach the end of the dough.
6. Eliminate all the extra parts from the edge of the dough, take a little bit of egg yolk, and stick the end of the dough into the location formed by the open edge of dough on the briwat. To position the folded edge correctly, make sure you utilize the tip of a butter knife.
7. Place the briwats in the refrigerator or cook them right away. The briwats should obtain a light golden brown color if you fry them in hot oil. You can also reheat the briwats in a 180 degrees Celsius oven if you want to serve them later on.
8. If you don't want to cook them now, you can place them in a refrigerator for 24 hours, or you can freeze them up for up to 8 weeks using a freezer bag or plastic storage container.

MOROCCAN TOMATO AND ROASTED PEPPER COOKED SALAD — TAKTOUKA

The list of ingredients you need:

- 50 g of finely chopped fresh cilantro
- 50 g of finely chopped fresh parsley
- Three big cloves of garlic, finely chopped and pressed
- Two or three big, fresh green peppers (roasted, peeled, seeded, and chopped)
- Six ripe fresh tomatoes (peeled, seeded, and chopped)
- Red pepper or pinch of cayenne
- 10 g cumin
- 15 g paprika
- 2 g black pepper
- 85ml olive oil

Preparation process

1. Take a large frying pan and combine all the ingredients. At medium to high heat, cook the ingredients for about twenty minutes while stirring frequently. In order to stop the tomatoes and peppers from burning, you can adjust the heat.
2. Keep on cooking for another 10 minutes after you smash the tomatoes with a spoon. In the end, ensure you stir the salad away from the sides of the pan to blend all the ingredients.
3. Adding crusty bread to your table is advised when serving taktouka!

MOROCCAN FAVA BEAN (BROAD BEAN) DIP — BESSARA

List of ingredients you need:

- 3 g sweet paprika
- 3 g hot paprika or cayenne pepper
- 30ml reserved cooking liquid
- 3 g salt
- 5 g ground cumin
- 150 g dried fava beans
- Two cloves garlic
- 80ml olive oil
- 65ml lemon juice
- Finely chopped parsley or cilantro
- Extra paprika, cumin, and olive oil

Preparation process

1. Use a big bowlful of water to soak the dried fava beans during the night time. Start by draining the beans and peeling them in the next day.
2. After you put the peeled fava beans in a large bowl, cover them with lots of water. Once the pot starts to boil, decrease the heat gradually, and simmer the beans until tender.
3. Keep the liquid obtained after draining the beans.
4. Put the beans into a food processor, and mix them with lemon juice, garlic, olive oil, two tablespoons of the reserved liquid, and spices. You need to obtain a smooth cream by processing the mix at high speed. If needed, you can add more liquid to thin the bessara.
5. This recipe should be served warm. Use the following ingredients to for garnishing: chopped parsley, paprika, hot paprika, olive oil, or ground cumin.

MOROCCAN ROASTED OR FRIED PEPPER SALAD

List of ingredients needed

- 3 g cumin
- 2 g salt, or more to taste
- Pepper
- 30ml lemon juice
- 30ml olive oil
- Four colored bell peppers (any color will do)

Preparation process

1. Chop the peppers in big pieces. Combine the pieces with the rest of the ingredients in a small frying pan. The peppers should get quite hot and the dressing really thick, so be careful how many minutes you sauté the mixture to make sure it doesn't burn.
2. After removing the pot from the stove, you will need to leave it for 30 minutes at room temperature to marinate.
3. You can serve the dish with crusty bread.

MOROCCAN ZAALOUK — EGGPLANT AND TOMATO COOKED SALAD

List of ingredients used

- 85ml water
- 60ml olive oil
- 1 g cayenne pepper
- 3 g salt
- 15 g paprika
- 100 g chopped fresh cilantro and parsley, combined
- Four large tomatoes, peeled, seeded, and chopped
- One big eggplant, peeled and chopped
- Small wedge of lemon

Preparation method

It will be far better to roast the eggplant instead of peeling and chopping it. Put the eggplant skin-side-up beneath a broiler after you slice it lengthwise. It should be left to roast until the skin is scorched and the eggplant is really tender. Take out the eggplant from the skin and use a vegetable masher to puree it.

How to prepare the zaalouk:

1. Use a large, deep skillet or pot to combine the ingredients. The next step would be to simmer over medium to high heat for a half hour, stirring from time to time. To avoid burning the zaalouk, you need to adjust the heat.

2. Crush and blend the tomatoes and eggplant by using a spoon or potato masher. At this point, you can add a small wedge of lemon to the combination. Keep on simmering to another 10 minutes so that the zaalouk can be stirred into a heap in the center of the pan.
3. Add crusty bread when serving.

MOROCCAN LENTILS — VEGETARIAN

List of ingredients

- 3 g ginger
- 10 g pepper
- 15 g paprika
- 15 g cumin
- 70 g chopped fresh parsley or cilantro
- Three cloves of garlic, finely chopped
- One medium onion, finely chopped
- 10 g salt
- 80ml olive oil
- 600 g lentils
- Two or Three tomatoes, grated

Preparation process

Take a pressure cooker or pot and combine all the ingredients. The next step is to add two liters of water.

Pressure cooker technique: The mixture should be covered and cooked for around half hour at medium heat. Reduce the liquids in case the lentils are still submerged in sauce at this point. Correct the seasoning according to your own taste with salt and pepper.

Pot technique: The lentils should be covered and simmered over medium heat for nearly two hours. You can add more water to the combination to prevent the lentils from burning. Correct the seasoning according to your taste again with salt and pepper.

You can use crusty bread to scoop up the lentils once the dish is done.

MOROCCAN FRIED EGGPLANT

List of ingredients

- 2 g pepper
- 3 g salt
- 3 g cumin
- 35 g flour
- Two eggs, lightly beaten
- Two medium narrow eggplants
- Vegetable oil

Preparation process

1. Cut off the ends of the eggplants after you wash them thoroughly. Try to obtain a striped effect by paring off some narrow strips of skin the full length of each eggplant.
2. Cut each eggplant in 2.5cm thick slices and set aside.
3. Blend the beaten eggs with the flour and spices in a mixing bowl. After you add the eggplant, stir to coat the slices properly.
4. Take a frying pan and cover its bottom with oil (about one quarter inch of oil) and then heat for a couple of minutes at medium heat. Fry the eggplant slices in batches as soon as the oil gets hot enough. Turn them a couple of times until they become tender and turn golden brown. Place them into a plate lined with paper towels to drain.
5. Leave them at room temperature before serving.
6. Place them eggplant in one layer on a baking sheet if you want to reheat it.

MOROCCAN GLAZED CARROTS

List of ingredients

- 35 g cilantro, chopped
- 30ml lemon juice
- 35 g sugar
- 50 mL olive oil
- 5 g salt
- 900 g carrots, peeled
- 5 g sweet red pepper, to taste

Directions

1. Take the carrots and slice them into long strips.
2. Put them in a pot with boiling water with salt and leave them until they become tender.
3. Put the rest of the ingredients in a bowl and mix them with the drained carrots.

RAGOUT OF CIPOLLINI ONIONS WITH TOMATO, CINNAMON, AND CUMIN

List of ingredients needed

- 70 g dried currants
- 250ml vegetable broth
- One cinnamon stick about 5cm long
- 2 g ground cumin
- 5 g ground coriander
- 900g cipollini onions, peeled
- 2 g ground black pepper, divided
- 3 g salt, divided
- 115 g tomatoes, sliced in half crosswise
- Cooking spray
- Two garlic cloves, nicely chopped
- 30g chopped fresh cilantro
- 5 g brown sugar
- 30ml fresh orange juice
- One orange rind strip 10cm long
- Two bay leaves
- Three thyme sprigs

Preparation process

1. Set the oven to 190 degrees Celsius to preheat it.
2. Coat the bottom of a 33x23cm baking dish with cooking spray and spread the garlic evenly across the dish. Place the tomato halves over the garlic. Sprinkle this combination with 1.38 g salt and 0.69 g pepper. Leave it to bake properly for approximately one hour. At the end, leave it to cool in dish.
3. Transfer the tomato mixture in a blender or food processor, keeping the liquid in the baking dish. Place the reserved liquid into a bowl.
4. Take a big nonstick skillet, coat it with cooking spray, and heat it over medium-high heat. Sauté it for around 10 minutes after adding the onions. Take out the onions from the pan. Sauté for another minute after you add coriander, cumin, and cinnamon to pan. Now add the pureed tomato mixture, onions, one quarter teaspoon salt, 0.69 g pepper, the leftover broth, and the following four ingredients to pan. Cook over medium heat for around half an hour, stirring from time to time. Stir in the orange juice and sugar after you remove it from heat. Sprinkle with cilantro after you have removed the cinnamon stick, bay leaves, and orange rind.

MAIN DISHES

MOROCCAN MEATBALL TAGINE WITH LEMON AND OLIVES

List of ingredients used

- 15ml tomato puree
- 250ml lamb stock
- Pinch saffron strands
- One red chili, deseeded and nicely chopped
- One slice (piece) of ginger of about 5cm, peeled and grated
- 30ml olive oil
- Tiny bunch flat-leaf parsley, chopped
- Pinch cayenne pepper
- 15 g ground cinnamon
- 15 g ground cumin
- Zest and juice from one unwaxed lemon, quartered
- 500g minced lamb
- Three onions, peeled
- Couscous or fresh crusty bread, for serving
- Tiny bunch coriander, chopped
- 100g pitted black kalamata olives

Preparation process

1. Place the onions in a blender and chop them very fine. Add the lemon zest, parsley, spices, lamb, and half the onions into a big bowl, and season. Mix the ingredients well by using your hands, and then shape the mixture into walnut-sized balls.
2. Use a big flameproof dish to heat the oil, and then add the rest of the onions, ginger, chili, and saffron. Take five minutes to cook it until the onion is softened. Now its time to add the lemon

juice, stock, tomato puree, and olives, and then bring it to a boil. Reduce the heat after you add the meatballs, one by one. Cook it for just about twenty minutes, constantly turning over the meatballs.

3. Tuck the coriander and lemon wedges in between the meatballs. Uncover the dish and cook for ten minutes until the remaining liquid has thickened slightly. Use crusty bread for serving.

AROMATIC LAMB WITH DATES

List of ingredients

- 50g of pitted dates
- 35 g coriander, roughly chopped
- 15ml tomato puree
- 35 g ground cinnamon
- 35 g ground coriander
- 300g sweet potatoes, cut into small chunks
- 500g diced boneless lean lamb
- One onion, chopped fine
- 15ml olive oil

Preparation process

1. Take a large pan and heat up the oil. The next step is to add the lamb and onion, and then fry until the lamb is lightly browned.
2. After adding the spices and sweet potatoes, take a moment to mix all the ingredients. Add 425ml boiling water and the tomato puree, and then leave the combination to boil.
3. Wait for about 15 minutes for the potatoes and lamb to grow tender, and then add the dates for another ten minutes. Serve with couscous after you sprinkle the recipe with coriander.

MOROCCAN SPICED FISH WITH GINGER MASH

List of ingredients

- Zest one lemon
- 15 g harissa
- One garlic clove, crushed
- 30ml butter, softened
- Two large sweet potatoes, peeled and cut into chunks
- Two white fish fillets, remove the skin
- One piece fresh root ginger of 2.5cm, nicely grated
- Tiny handful coriander, mostly chopped, the rest left whole

Preparation process

1. Prepare and heat oven to 200 degrees Celsius. Put some salt in the boiling water and cook the sweet potatoes for ten minutes or until they get really tender. In the same time, combine the butter with the garlic, harissa, lemon zest, and chopped coriander. At the end, drain the potatoes completely, mash with ginger and seasoning, and maintain a warm temperature in the dish.
2. Transfer the fish into a roasting tin, season, and then spread half the flavored butter over each fillet. Cook for nearly 8 minutes until just cooked through.

MOROCCAN PIGEON PIE (BESTILLA)

List of ingredients

- 50 g minced parsley
- 50 g minced cilantro
- 5 g saffron threads, combined with 15ml water
- 10 g rushed red chile flakes
- 15 g ras el hanout
- One medium yellow onion, minced
- Four cloves garlic, minced
- 45ml olive oil
- Three eggs
- 750ml chicken stock
- 1.4 Kg pigeon or bone-in, skin-on chicken thighs
- 125 g blanched almonds
- 5 g ground cinnamon
- 70 g confectioners' sugar
- 8 sheet phyllo dough
- 100 g unsalted butter, melted, plus more
- Salt and freshly ground black pepper, to taste

Preparation process

1. Take five minutes to toast the almonds in a four quart saucepan over medium-high heat. Put them in a food processor after they have cooled down and pulse until ground. Add pigeon and stock to pan and let them boil. The heat should be set to medium-low for this process: cook (covered) until pigeons are cooked completely. This should take about three quarters of an hour. Place the pigeons

onto a cutting board with tongs and shred the meat. Simmer cooking liquid over medium heat until reduced to one cup, for half hour. Let it cool down and whisk in eggs. Put the sauce aside.

2. Put some oil in a clean pan and let it heat. Place the garlic and onion in it and cook until golden, about ten minutes. Next you need to add ras el hanout, chile flakes, and saffron mixture, cook 1-2 minutes and then remove from heat. Stir in the remainder of the almonds, shredded meat, and sauce, the cilantro, parsley, salt, and pepper. Put the filling in a different bowl.

3. The oven should be heated to 200 degrees Celsius. Use butter to grease a 23cm spring form pan. Put one sheet phyllo on a work surface and brush with melted butter. Position it into pan, allowing corners to hang over the sides. Do the same thing with the second sheet phyllo. Spread one third of the filling over dough. Perform this process of layering a couple of times more. Fold corners of phyllo over filling. Top with remaining 2 sheets buttered phyllo, tuck corners around sides of pan, encasing the filling. Bake until golden and filling is set, for half hour. Let cool slightly, then unmold. Dust with confectioners` sugar and cinnamon.

MROUZIA (HONEY-BRAISED LAMB SHANKS)

List of ingredients

- One stick cinnamon
- 5 g crushed saffron threads
- 35 g ras el hanout
- 300 g golden raisins
- One large white onion, finely chopped
- Salt and freshly ground black pepper, to taste
- Four lamb shanks, frenched, if desired
- 50 g unsalted butter
- 60ml olive oil
- One stick cinnamon
- 300 g blanched whole almonds
- Toasted sesame seeds, to garnish
- 170ml honey

Preparation process

1. Use a large pot to heat the oil and butter (a Dutch oven works well if you have one available) over medium-high heat. Use salt and pepper to season the lamb, and then cook. Turn the meat around as necessary and until it gets a brown color all over, for approximately 12 minutes. Place the meat onto a plate and set aside.
2. The next step will be to add onion to the pot, and cook, stirring, until soft, for nearly five minutes. Now add ras el hanout, saffron, raisins, and cinnamon, and cook, stirring until fragrant, for a couple of minutes. Add lamb, almonds, honey, and three cups water, and bring to a boil. Reduce heat to medium, and cook, partially covered, until the lamb is really tender, for 1 hour and 30 minutes. Split the shanks and sauce among serving plates, and sprinkle each with sesame seeds.

MOROCCAN MEATBALLS WITH ARUGULA

List of ingredients

- 30ml olive oil
- Salt and ground black pepper, to taste
- Nine cloves garlic, six minced, Three peeled and crushed
- 15 g dried oregano
- 400 g minced mint
- 150 g minced parsley
- 900g ground lamb
- One half whole wheat 20cm pitas, torn into 2.5cm pieces
- 125ml milk
- Sixteen cherry tomatoes, halved
- 2000ml baby arugula
- 150 g roughly chopped basil
- 15ml fresh lemon juice
- 170ml Greek yogurt
- 125ml vegetable oil
- Two egg yolks
- 10 g harissa
- One can whole peeled tomatoes, crushed by hand

Preparation process

Use a bowl to mix milk and pita. Leave it at room temperature for five minutes. The next step is to add lamb, one cup of the parsley, the mint, oregano, and one quarter of the minced garlic, salt, and pepper. You will need to divide into 36, 30 g balls, so be careful when mixing the ingredients. Use a medium to large-sized saucepan to heat half the olive oil over medium-high heat. Cook meatballs until they get a brown color (5 minutes) while working in batches. Put the remaining olive oil into pan, returning to medium-high heat. Cook crushed garlic for a couple of minutes. Add tomatoes, harissa, salt, and pepper. Simmer until sauce is slightly thickened, for six minutes. Add the remaining meatballs. Cover and cook until they are tender, for one quarter hour. Use a bowl to whisk the remaining minced garlic, the egg yolks, salt, and pepper in a bowl. Whisk while drizzling in canola oil until the mixture is emulsified, creating an aioli. Whisk in yogurt and lemon juice and then drizzle aioli mixture over meatballs. Use the remaining parsley and the basil to garnish the recipe. Tomatoes and arugula are great for a garnish.

SPICED LAMB SAUSAGES

List of ingredients

- 5 g ground fennel seed
- 10 g ground cumin
- 10 g ground coriander
- 15 g paprika
- 15 minced flat-leaf parsley
- Three cloves garlic, nicely chopped
- 15 g harissa
- 455g trimmed lamb shoulder, cut into 2.5cm cubes, or 455g ground lamb
- Flat bread, for serving
- Chopped tomatoes, red onions, and cucumbers, for serving
- Eight leaves of basil, roughly chopped
- 125ml yogurt
- 60ml extra-virgin olive oil
- Salt and freshly ground black pepper, to taste

Preparation process

1. You will need to use a food processor for this recipe. Take the lamb and place it into the bowl of the processor. Fit the processor properly with a chopping blade and then put it all in a freezer for half hour. Take it out and put harissa, two cloves garlic, parsley, coriander, paprika, cumin, fennel, salt, and pepper into the bowl. Process until lamb is coarsely chopped and mixed with spices, about fifteen seconds. Split lamb mixture into 8 portions and form the portions into 8 cm wide patties. Heat 30ml oil in a 30 cm cast-iron skillet over medium-high heat. Add lamb patties and cook, turning once until browned and still slightly pink, for seven minutes. Transfer to paper towels and set aside.

2. During this time, stir the remaining garlic and oil, yogurt, and basil in a tiny bowl to make a sauce. Season with salt and pepper. Use sauce, chopped vegetables, and flat bread and serve with the patties on a platter.

STRIPED BASS STUFFED WITH SWORDFISH AND SHRIMP

List of ingredients

- 100 g finely chopped fresh parsley
- 15 g ground cumin
- 10 g paprika
- 5 g cayenne
- 5 g freshly ground white pepper
- 60ml fresh lemon juice
- 60ml extra-virgin olive oil
- 40 g coarse salt
- Two whole farm-raised striped bass
- Pinch ground turmeric
- 6 g ground ginger
- 115g raw small shrimp, peeled, deveined, and cut in half
- 10 cloves garlic, peeled and finely chopped
- 100 g nicely chopped fresh cilantro
- 70 g finely diced celery

Preparation process

1. Use one tablespoon of the salt to rub the fish inside and out after you rinse them. Leave them on the table for twenty minutes.
2. Take a grill or broiler and heat it to high. Combine one tablespoon of the oil, two tablespoons of the lemon juice, half tablespoon of the salt, and one quarter tablespoon of the white pepper in a tiny bowl, and then put the mixture over the fish inside and out. Cut fish crosswise on both sides, but be careful not to slice through the bones. Mix two tablespoons of the oil, one tablespoon of the lemon juice, cayenne, and paprika, one quarter tablespoon of the cumin, parsley, celery, cilantro,

garlic, swordfish, and shrimp in a medium bowl and mix properly. Use the swordfish mixture to stuff the cavity and then brush the outsides with any remaining liquid.

3. Use the remaining tablespoon oil to brush fish and position it in an oiled fish rack to maintain the stuffing inside when turning. Take eight minutes to grill or broil the fish on each side.

4. Take another tiny bowl and mix the remaining one quarter teaspoon of salt, half teaspoon white pepper and three quarters teaspoon cumin, ginger, and turmeric. Use spices to sprinkle fish and the remaining lemon juice to drizzle on top. Serve with olive oil on the side.

LENTILS WITH SWISS CHARD AND KHLEA

List of ingredients

- Ground black pepper
- Juice obtained from one lemon
- 150 g nicely chopped fresh cilantro
- 75 g finely chopped fresh parsley
- Two fresh plum tomatoes, cut in half inch dice
- 15 g seven-spice mixture
- Salt to taste
- Two cloves garlic, peeled and crushed
- Two medium sized red onions, peeled and finely chopped
- 340g Swiss chard
- 450 g small brown lentils
- Ten pieces khlea

Preparation method

1. Take khlea and scrape solidified oil from it for 30ml total. Take a small bowl, shred the meat into large pieces and cover the pieces with water.
2. Select the lentils and rinse them. Put them in a big, heavy saucepan, cover with water, and then bring them to a boiling point slowly. Return to saucepan after you drain lentils. Add two and half cups of cold water and simmer over low heat for twenty minutes, removing any foam. During this time, split the ribs from chard leaves and chop them both. Add to lentils and simmer for additional twenty minutes. In the end the lentils must be tender. Set lentil mixture aside after you have removed the excess liquid.

3. Take a big skillet and heat the reserved oil in medium heat. Add the onions and cook for approximately twenty minutes. Add garlic, spice mixture, and pinch of salt and cook two minutes longer. Stir in drained khlea, tomatoes, 34.62 g of the parsley, and 60ml of the cilantro.
4. Add lentil mixture to skillet and cook over medium to low heat for ten minutes. Take the skillet away from the heat source and let it sit at room temperature, covered, for fifteen minutes. Use salt, pepper, and lemon juice to season to taste. Top with the remaining 34.62 g parsley and one quarter cup cilantro and serve.

DJEJ MECHOUI (GRILLED CHICKEN WITH MOROCCAN SPICES)

List of ingredients needed

- 70 g butter, softened
- 10 g ground cumin
- One pinch hot paprika
- 15 g sweet paprika
- 5 g salt
- 35 g fresh parsley, chopped
- 35 g fresh cilantro, chopped
- One clove garlic, peeled
  Three scallions, white ends only, chopped
- Four poussins or two small chickens

Preparation process

1. Take a moment to crush the garlic, parsley, cilantro, scallions, hot paprika, salt, sweet paprika, and cumin with a mortar and pestle. Mix in the butter.
2. Split the poultry down the back and flatten. Rub inside and out with butter paste and leave them on the table for about 45 minutes.
3. Place the poultry skin side up on the preheated grill. Flip it over after two minutes and baste with any extra paste. Keep on flipping and baste to the point when skin is crisp and flesh is firm.

SWEET AND SAVORY SQUAB AND ALMOND PIE

List of ingredients

- 15 g ground cinnamon
- Two 450g squabs
- Salt and freshly ground white pepper
- Pinch saffron threads
- 5ml ground ginger
- One cinnamon stick
- Two medium onions, peeled and nicely chopped
- 60ml olive oil
- Confectioners` sugar
- 185ml clarified butter
- Ten sheets phyllo dough
- 200 g sliced almonds, toasted and lightly crushed with a rolling pin
- 15 g sugar
- 50 g minced fresh parsley
- Two eggs, lightly beaten
- 60ml orange-flower water

Preparation process

1. Take a deep pan and heat olive oil over medium heat. Add onions and cook for five minutes. Add ginger, saffron, cinnamon stick, and pepper and salt according to your likes. Add 80ml water, and then place squabs breast side down in pan. Minimize heat to low and cook, covered, for half hour, turning the squabs once.
2. Take squabs from pan and let them cool. Simmer onion mixture, uncovered, to the point where pan juices are cut to half, about ten minutes. Eliminate the skin and bones with your hands

when squabs are cool enough. Put the meat in a bowl, and then stir in 5ml cinnamon and 5ml orange-flower water. Put squab mixture aside.

3. Break eggs into the reduced pan juices, and then add the remaining 10ml cinnamon, parsley, sugar, 15ml orange-flower water, and almonds. Cook to the point where eggs have scrambled and absorbed all juices, so that consistency is somewhat dry, which will take a couple of minutes. Take away from the heat source and leave it at room temperature.

4. Put one sheet phyllo on a clean surface and brush with butter. Put a second sheet over it and brush with butter. Put buttered sheets centered over an 20cm plate. Redo this process three times, putting each pair of sheets at an angle over previous sheets to create an irregular bottom crust. Position squab mixture on crust and top with the almond mixture. Fold overhanging bottoms sheets over to enclose filling totally. Use clarified butter to brush the top to seal.

5. Use a nonstick frying pan in order to heat two tablespoons clarified butter over medium heat. Place the phyllo pockets into pan and fry until sides are golden brown color, for about three minutes. Flip the pockets and fry about another two minutes. Place it on a serving plate and sprinkle with confectioners' sugar.

COUSCOUS ROYALE (COUSCOUS WITH GRILLED MEATS)

List of ingredients needed

For the grilled meat:

- One egg
- One bunch cilantro, minced
- One small onion, grated
- Six cloves garlic, minced
- 50 g ground cumin
- 455g ground lamb
- Eight merguez sausages
- Eight baby lamb chops
- 455g boneless, skinless chicken thighs, sliced into pieces
- Salt and freshly ground black pepper, to taste

For the stew:

- One medium zucchini, sliced into 2.5cm pieces
- One medium white turnip, peeled and sliced into 2.5cm pieces
- One medium yellow onion, roughly chopped
- Two small red Holland chiles, stemmed, seeded, and chopped
- Two ribs celery, roughly chopped
- Two medium carrots, peeled and cut into slices about a half centimeter thick
- Four cloves garlic, chopped
- 150 g flour
- Salt and freshly ground black pepper, to taste
- 340g boneless lamb shoulder, trimmed and sliced into 2.5cm pieces

- 80ml olive oil
- Juice from one lemon
- One bunch parsley, chopped
- One small head cabbage, cored and chopped
- One can whole peeled tomatoes in juice, crushed by hand
- 300 g dried chickpeas, soaked for at least 8 hours and drained
- 1L chicken stock
- Two bay leaves
- Two sticks cinnamon
- 2 g crushed saffron threads
- 3 g ground ginger
- 5 g paprika
- 35 g tomato paste
- 150 golden raisins

For the couscous:

- Harissa, for serving
- 70 g unsalted butter
- 45ml olive oil
- 850 g fine-grain couscous

Preparation process

1. After marinating the meat, take a bowl and mix the following ingredients: ground lamb, one and half tablespoon paprika, one and half tablespoon cumin, half the garlic, onion, three quarter of the cilantro, egg, and salt and pepper. Form the mixture into twelve oval balls, about 30g each, and place three balls on 20cm wooden skewers. Put the skewers on a plate and refrigerate to the point when you can put it on the grill. Add the remaining paprika, cumin, garlic, and cilantro in a bowl, add chicken and lamb chops, and season with salt and pepper. Mix the ingredients well by tossing. Place it in the fridge for 60 minutes and ensure you cover the bowl.

2. Prepare the stew: Take a large saucepan and heat oil over medium high heat. Use salt and pepper to season lamb, dredge in flour, and cook, flipping as needed, until browned all over, for six minutes. Transfer meat to a bowl using a slotted spoon and set it aside. Add, celery, chiles, carrots, garlic, onion, turnip, and zucchini to saucepan, and cook, stirring, until golden brown, for twelve minutes. Add saffron, raisins, saffron, cinnamon, tomato paste, paprika, ginger, and bay leaves, and cook, stirring, until lightly caramelized, for three minutes. Place lamb into the pan with stock, chickpeas, tomatoes, and cabbage, and bring to boil. Decrease heat to medium, and cook, covered and stirring from time to time, until meat and chickpeas are really tender, for approximately two and half hours. Use salt and pepper to season the dish, and stir in parsley and juice.
3. Prepare the couscous: take butter, oil, and six cups water to boil over high heat. Stir in couscous, season with salt and pepper, and cover. Take it away from the heat source, and let sit until water is totally absorbed, for ten minutes. Use a fork to fluff couscous, set apart in a warm place.
4. Use a charcoal grill and build a medium-hot fire, or heat a gas grill to medium-high. Take away chicken out of the marinade, split and thread among four more wooden skewers, and working in batches, add to grill. Cook, turning once, until charred in spots and cooked through, for ten minutes. Place in a serving platter, and redo the process with lamb skewers, lamb chops, and sausages, about sixteen minutes for the lamb skewers, about seven minutes for lamb chops, and about eighteen minutes for sausages. Serve stew, couscous, and grilled meats together on the table with harissa on the side.

DESSERTS

MHANNCHA (THE SNAKE)

The list of ingredients

- Eight sheets phyllo pastry
- 5 g ground cinnamon
- 15 g butter, melted
- 10ml orange flower water
- Butter
- Ground cinnamon
- Icing sugar
- 150g chopped almonds
- 75g granulated sugar

Preparation process

1. Use a blender to obtain a smooth mixture of sugar, orange flower water, butter, almonds and cinnamon.
2. Split the mixture into eight equal portions and place each of them lengthways down the side of one piece of phyllo pastry. Roll the pastry over the mixture. You should obtain some sort of a sausage shape in the end.
3. You need to roll the sausage shape into the shape of a snail's shell by coiling the mixture and then cover it with a damp tea towel to keep moist. Redo this process for all eight pieces.
4. Use a large pan to heat the butter and then take the pastries and fry them until they are browned on both sides.
5. Use cinnamon and icing sugar to sprinkle the pastries and serve. These can be eaten warm or cold.

HAROST BALLS

List of ingredients needed

- 150 g of dark raisins
- 150 g golden raisins
- 600 g pitted dates
- 15ml or 30ml Zinfandel wine (non-alcoholic wine is a perfect substitute)
- 150 g walnuts

Preparation process

1 Use a food blender to mix dates, raisins, and walnuts until the contents are nicely chopped and start to stick together.
2. Mix in the wine and stir well until the mixture gets a sticky texture.
3. Split the mixture into tiny sections with a spoon and place them onto a sheet of wax paper; roll these pieces into balls.
4. Place them in a refrigerator for a minimum of three hours before serving.

A special note: If you wish to use a wine substitute altogether, many different liquids can work quite well. I recommend using pomegranate or red grape juice for a bit sweeter flavor, and using white grape juice or chicken stock for more savory flavor. This applies not only to this recipe, but any time you need a great substitute for wine!

MOROCCAN CAKE

List of ingredients

- 15 g baking powder
- 850 g flour
- 250ml oil
- 150 g sugar
- Five eggs
- 170g container of vanilla yogurt

Preparation process

1. Take a bowl and combine the yogurt with the flour and sugar. Add the oil, baking powder, and eggs and stir. Make sure the ingredients are blended well.
2. Place into a cake tin and heat the oven to 180 degrees Celsius. Cook the cake for about half hour until a toothpick inserted in the center comes out clean.

SFINJ — MOROCCAN DOUGHNUTS

List of ingredients

- 30 g baker's yeast
- 1 kg sifted flour
- 5 g salt

Preparation process

1. Take a glass of lukewarm water to dissolve the yeast.
2. Combine the flour, salt, and yeast within the glass of lukewarm water when the yeast is dissolved. Then, knead to the point where the dough is soft and elastic.
3. Position the dough into a bowl and cover with a cloth. Let it rest for around three and half hours.
4. Roll pieces of the dough into tiny ropes and connect the ends of the ropes to form rings. Put a little bit of oil on your hands before you start rolling. Once
5. Drop the rings into a pan of hot oil.
6. When they obtain a brown color, take them out and serve hot. Use sugar or honey to dust or coat them.

MOROCCAN DATE PUDDING

List of ingredients needed

- 3 g ground cloves
- 50 g roughly chopped walnuts
- 3 g vanilla extract
- 120ml milk
- 5 g nutmeg
- 5 g cinnamon
- 125g plain white flour
- 5 g baking powder
- Four eggs
- 125g caster sugar
- 125g butter

Preparation process

1. Grease a 20cm cake tin after you preheat your oven to 165 degrees Celsius.
2. Take a large bowl and combine the butter and sugar until blended and fluffy.
3. Before you add eggs to the butter and sugar, you need to beat the eggs in a separate small bowl. Once beaten, add the eggs to the butter and sugar.
4. Combine the baking powder, flour, cinnamon, nutmeg, and cloves in a second big bowl.
5. Combine the ingredients in the two bowls and beat well. Add the milk and vanilla and beat again in order to ensure that the mixture is smooth and even.
6. Now is the time to add the chopped dates and walnuts, and stir again to ensure that they are equally distributed.
7. Place the mixture into the prepared cake tin and bake for half hour or until a toothpick inserted in the center comes out clean.

BAKLAVA

List of ingredients

- 30ml fresh lemon juice
- 455g unsalted butter, melted
- One stick cinnamon
- 40 sheets phyllo dough
- 20 g ground cinnamon
- 100 g bread crumbs
- 1300 g sugar
- 1500 g finely chopped blanched almonds

Preparation process

1. Heat your oven to 150 degrees Celsius and then mix almonds, 144.24 g sugar, bread crumbs, and ground cinnamon in a large bowl. Set filling aside. Unwrap phyllo and slice to fit in a 30 x 40 cm baking pan. Use a damp dish towel to cover phyllo sheets to keep them moist.
2. Use melted butter to grease a baking pan. Brush the pan with butter and place one sheet of phyllo on it. Place the second sheet of phyllo over first sheet, brush with butter, and then sprinkle with two tablespoons almond filling evenly on the dough. Place a sheet of phyllo out on a clean work surface, brush with butter and transfer to pan with the buttered side up. Use almond mixture and sprinkle it evenly on this sheet. Place the 2 sheets of phyllo apart for the top, and then keep on alternating the almond mixture with single buttered sheets of phyllo. Cover the very top with the one last phyllo sheet.
3. Use butter to brush top of the baklava. Use a serrated knife at about two inch intervals to cut across baklava in order to obtain eight equal strips. Use water to sprinkle the baklava, cover with two sheets of parchment paper, and bake until golden, about one and half hours.

4. The remaining four cups sugar, juice, cinnamon stick, and two cups water should be heated in a saucepan over medium heat. Cook until sugar dissolves; this will take about fifteen minutes. Take off the heat, and discard the cinnamon stick.
5. Take the baklava out of the oven and place on parchment paper, and then pour the syrup over all of the baklava. The syrup must reach all corners, so make sure you tilt the pan.

KAAB GHZAL - GAZELLE HORNS (CORNES DE GAZELLE)

List of ingredients

For the almond paste

- 2 g cinnamon
- 60ml unsalted butter, melted
- 80ml orange flower water
- 90 g sugar
- Tiny pinch of mastic or gum Arabic powder
- 455g blanched almonds

For the pastry dough

- 200 g unsalted butter, melted
- 60ml or 75ml orange flower water
- Two small eggs
- 850 g flour
- 3 g salt

For the optional egg wash

- 15ml orange flower water
- One egg

Prepare the almond paste

1. A meat grinder should be used to grind the almonds into a paste. You can also use a food processor to grind the almonds for a couple of minutes until a paste forms.
2. Combine sugar, cinnamon, orange, flower water, and gum Arabic powder with the ground almonds using your hands.
3. Grab a part of the almond paste mixture and shape it into short sticks that look like sausages. They should be really small in size, about 5cm long. Cover and place aside. (You can also refrigerate the almond paste for a couple of days).

Prepare the Kaab Ghzal

1. Use flour to prepare your working surface. Take a portion of dough and roll it until it gets really thin. Lift up the dough and reposition it a couple of times in order to ease the rolling-out.
2. Place a stick of paste close to the top of the dough. Conceal the almond paste with the dough. Two or more sticks of paste can be arranged before folding over the dough, according to the width of the dough you have rolled out. When you do this, make sure you allow about one centimeter between the sticks.
3. With your fingers, mold the concealed almond pace into a crescent shape with the outer curve facing you. When you bake the cookies, they will swell a little bit, and so you need to mold the cookies so that they appear a little bit narrow.
4. Use a pastry wheel or knife to cut the crescent which will seal the edges together. You should also pinch the dough to properly enclose the almond paste. Place the cookies on an ungreased baking sheet.
5. Use the remaining dough and paste to redo the process above. Leave any unused dough under the plastic wrap. While you work, collect the dough scraps, shape them into balls, and return to the plastic to rest before rolling out the dough again.

Prepare the cookies

1. You must leave the shaped cookies untouched for an hour before baking.
2. Heat your oven to 180 degrees Celsius.
3. A really attractive sheen is provided to the baked cookies by the additional egg wash. Beat 1 egg with 15ml of orange flower water to prepare the egg wash. Cover the cookies with the egg wash.
4. Place the cookies in the middle of the oven and bake for twelve minutes.

FRIED MOROCCAN HONEY CAKES

List of ingredients needed

FOR THE CAKES

- 185g flour
- 70 g powdered sugar
- 5 g baking powder
- 60ml vegetable oil
- 15 g orange zest, finely grated
- Three eggs

FOR SYRUP

- 15 g orange zest, nicely grated
- 80ml honey
- 400 g sugar
- 30ml lemon juice
- 310ml water
- Vegetable oil for frying

Preparation process

1. Take a large bowl and whisk the eggs, orange juice, and oil in it. Mix with the orange zest and sugar, and then whisk until frothy.
2. Use a spoon to mix this mixture with the flour and baking powder. Cover the bowl and leave it on the table for 60 minutes.

3. You will need to heat water with lemon juice and sugar in a saucepan to create the syrup. Make sure to stir properly until sugar dissolves. When it reaches a boiling point, decrease the heat and simmer for five minutes. For the following five minutes, you will need to add the honey and orange zest as well. Maintain the temperature at a simmer.
4. Transfer the dough into a lightly floured surface after you sprinkle some flour onto it. The dough should not stick to your hands, so make sure you use enough flour.
5. The dough should then be rolled out until it is 1/2cm thick. You have to continue rolling the dough and rest until it stops shrinking back, since it is quite elastic.
6. Cut out round shapes using a two inch cookie cutter.
7. Take a large deep-sided frying pan and heat the oil to 160 degrees Celsius. The cakes should be fried for a couple of minutes on each side until golden.
8. Dip the cakes into the warm syrup with the help of some tongs. Move to a serving platter. You can eat them warm or cold.

BREADS

BEGHRIR — CREPE-LIKE MOROCCAN SEMOLINA PANCAKES

List of ingredients used

Conventional measures

- 15 g yeast
- 780ml lukewarm water
- 35 g baking powder
- 5 g sugar
- 5 g salt
- 200 g all-purpose flour
- 425 g fine semolina

Traditional Moroccan Measures

- One teaspoon salt
- Half glass all purpose flour
- One level glass of the semolina
- Two glasses lukewarm water
- One tablespoon yeast
- Two tablespoons baking powder
- One teaspoon sugar

Preparation process

Prepare the butter

1. Take a mixing bowl and combine the flour, semolina, salt, sugar, and baking powder. Put 750ml of lukewarm water in a blender.
2. Introduce the yeast and process on low speed to blend. Take time to include the dry ingredients into the blender step by step.
3. Blend for 1 minute after you increase the processing speed. Now the butter should be rather thin.
4. Take a bowl and pour the batter in it. Set the bowl aside for ten minutes after you have covered it with plastic wrap.

Prepare the Beghrir

1. Take a non-stick skillet and heat it over medium heat. Take a ladle to pour the batter into the hot skillet. The batter should spread evenly into a circle if you pour carefully and slowly. However, the batter should spread itself, so don't swirl the pan as you would for a crepe. The beghrir should be made as large as possible.
2. You should notice some bubbles at the surface of the beghrir as it starts to cook. It will simply get cooked on one side so don't flip it.
3. You need to cook the beghrir for a couple of minutes until it gets cooked on one side. When you touch the beghrir, it should feel spongy.
4. Place the beghrir to cool in one layer on a clean kitchen towel. They can get easily stacked without sticking once they cool down.
5. Do the same with the remaining batter to create more beghrir.

MOROCCAN HONEYCOMB PANCAKES

List of ingredients

- 600 g fine semolina
- 600 g lukewarm milk
- 650 g lukewarm water
- One egg
- 5 g sugar
- 5 g salt
- 15 g baking powder
- 15 g yeast
- 300 g all purpose flour

Preparation process

1. Use a blender mix all ingredients for 1 minute until you obtain a thin, smooth batter. Place the batter in a bowl, use plastic wrap to cover it, and set aside for a couple of hours until the batter has risen a bit and the top is bubbly and foamy. You have to combine the ingredients in a bowl first, and then process the batter in batches in the blender in case the machine does not have at least 1500 ml in capacity.
2. Take a non-stick skillet and heat it over medium heat. In order to reduce the total cooking time, you can use two pans. Make use of a ladle to pour batter into the hot skillet while stirring the batter. The batter will spread evenly into a circle only if you pour carefully and slowly into the center.
3. You should notice some bubbles at the surface of the beghrir as it starts to cook. It will simply get cooked on one side so don't flip it.
4. You need to cook the beghrir for a couple of minutes until it gets cooked on 1 side. When you touch the beghrir, it should feel spongy.

5. Place the beghrir to cool in one layer on a clean kitchen towel. They can get easily stacked without sticking after they cool down.
6. Do the same with the remaining batter.
7. Syrup made from butter and honey is usually used to serve beghrir. You should heat equal amounts of butter and honey until bubbly and hot, and then dip the beghrir in the syrup. Serve immediately after you roll them up on a serving plate.

KRACHEL — MOROCCAN SWEET ROLLS WITH ANISE AND SESAME

List of ingredients

- Two eggs, lightly beaten
- 10 g anise seeds
- 10 g salt
- 150 g sugar
- 1300 g flour
- 190ml warm milk
- 30ml orange flower water
- 30ml vegetable oil
- 125ml melted butter
- 15 g unhulled, golden sesame seeds
- Egg wash made from one egg beaten with 15ml milk

Preparation process

1. Use a small quantity of warm milk to dissolve the yeast and set aside.
2. Mix the flour, salt, and anise seeds in a big bowl. Include the eggs, butter, oil, orange flower water, yeast, and the rest of the milk. Combine to form really soft, sticky dough.
3. In case the dough is too sticky to handle, you can add some flour in order to make it manageable.
4. Use a lightly floured surface to knead the dough.
5. Place the dough on an oiled bowl and flip it over once to cover it with oil. Use a towel to cover the bowl and set aside to rise until doubled. Make sure you leave it there for at least 2 hours.
6. The next step would be to create between 12 and 15 smooth, evenly shaped balls out of the dough. Transfer the balls onto an oiled baking sheet, two inches apart.

7. Use a towel to cover the baking sheet and leave the dough to rise another hour or longer, or until the rolls are really light and puffy.
8. Heat your oven to 230 degrees Celsius. Use the egg wash to brush the tops and sides of the rolls. Use sesame seeds to sprinkle the rolls.
9. The krachel should be baked for around a half an hour. Once done, place the rolls on a rack and let them cool.

SFENJ — MOROCCAN DOUGHNUTS OR FRITTERS

List of ingredients

- 315ml warm water
- 5 g salt
- 10 g yeast
- 875 g flour
- Vegetable oil for frying
- You can also use sugar for garnish

Preparation process

1. Use warm water to dissolve the yeast and place apart.
2. Use a large bowl to mix the flour and salt. Include the water and yeast mixture and stir with your hand until smooth. At this point, you will find the dough to be too sticky to knead.
3. The dough should be left to rise for about 4 hours, until it doubles or triples in size.
4. You should heat an inch of vegetable oil in a wide pot. Try pulling off a piece of dough about the size of a small plum after you dip your hand in water. You have to make a hole in the ball of dough, stretch it wide, and place dough in the hot oil. The holes must be done with your fingers.
5. Do the same thing with the rest of the dough, continually wetting your hands if required.
6. The sfenj should be fried until it gets a golden brown color. Transfer the cooked sfenj to a plate lines with paper towels to drain.
7. The sfenj should be served hot. You can also dip them in sugar if you want to.

MOROCCAN ONION FLATBREAD

Dough

- 5 g salt
- 80ml olive oil
- 1300 g all-purpose flour
- 440ml lukewarm water
- One packet active dry yeast

Combine the yeast, ¾ cup warm water, and ½ cup of flour in a bowl of a large stand mixer, with the help of a whisk. It will take almost five minutes for the mixture to get foamy. The next step would be to add the remaining four cups of flour, salt, olive oil, and the remaining cup of warm water to activate the yeast. Make use of the dough hood attachment and mix until the dough gathers into a smooth ball. This should be done in speed setting two on the mixer. Let it rest in the refrigerator during the night

Spicy Onion Filling

- 5 g Spanish smoked paprika
- 5 g black pepper
- 10 g paprika
- Half Rocoto chili pepper, seeds removed and finely chopped
- 5 g coriander seeds, toaster and ground
- 5 g cumin seeds, toasted and ground
- 35 g butter
- 30ml olive oil
- Four medium onions, thinly sliced
- 60ml dry white wine (or non-alcoholic substitute - see above)

- 35 g chopped cilantro
- 35 g chopped parsley

1. Heat your oven to 200 degrees Celsius. Add the olive oil and sliced onions in a big, heavy skillet and cook. The onions should get a golden brown color so you need to stir occasionally. Use 60ml of white wine (or substitute) to de-glaze the pan and then add the cumin, coriander, chopped red chile, paprika, Spanish paprika, black pepper, and salt. Take the onions off from the heat and use chopped parsley and cilantro to sprinkle on the onions.
2. Split the dough into six equal sized balls and cover and let rise for an extra ten minutes. Roll out two of the dough balls into six to eight inch rounds, and then place 1/3 of the onion mixture on one of the rounds with a spoon. Use the other round to cover and pinch the edges together. Use your hands to flatten out the dough and carefully roll out the 30cm circle. Make sure the onion filling does not split out the sides. Make 2 more flatbreads with the remaining dough and onion mixture.
3. Transfer the flatbreads to three separate lightly greased baking sheets with a wide spatula and your hands. Bake them for just about 20 minutes. Flip the bread halfway through. Use coarse salt to sprinkle and olive oil to brush, and then serve at room temperature.

CONCLUSION

Moroccan cuisine incorporates an incredible variety of dishes as you've seen in this book. Taking elements from many cultures and cuisines, it is truly delicious food any time of day!

Moroccan cuisine is also very healthy. The dishes are meat-based but with plenty of vegetables in each dish. The dishes are flavored with herbs and spices that not only taste good, but are also beneficial for your health. The recipes are very easy to make, they are also very quick especially if you use a tagine (clay pot).

Moroccan cuisine is amazing and you will not be disappointed with exotic and amazing tastes. Enjoy it with your friends and family, and experience meals you won't forget in a hurry!

Lastly, if you've enjoyed this book, I would sincerely appreciate a review of the book on Amazon. Thank you so much and enjoy your Moroccan meals!

Printed in Poland
by Amazon Fulfillment
Poland Sp. z o.o., Wrocław